Being a Product Manager

SHALINI SAHAY

Copyright © 2012 Shalini Sahay

All rights reserved.

ISBN: 97983737965

DEDICATION

To all my wonderful readers:
who dream of excelling in their careers and
becoming great leaders, not only professionally but
personally as well.

Special thanks to my former manager Samir Paul,
who is not only my mentor but an inspirational
leader too. His constant guidance and willingness to
share his vast knowledge helped me to achieve this.

CONTENTS

	Acknowledgments	i
1	Why	Pg 5
2	Ideation	Pg 13
3	Strategy	Pg 17
4	Roadmap	Pg 23
5	Planning	Pg 29
6	Design & Development	Pg 36
7	Launch	Pg 41
8	Epilogue	Pg 47
	About the author	Pg 50

ACKNOWLEDGMENTS

I am introducing my first piece of work. The book is based on the phycological skills, interpersonal skills, and emotional intelligence of a product manager.

Many people reached out to me with numerous questions about product management, and the most common of all was,
"Which certification helps a professional to become a product manager?"

As a result, I set out to come up with a piece of work that can answer this question simply but effectively.

The answer is very simple. There are many certifications that a professional can take up to try for the role of a product manager. However, a product manager is not just a title that can be achieved by clearing a theoretical exam.

Product management is a mindset - a mindset to be honest and perspicuous, a mindset to be attentive and conscientious to your organization and your customers.

Being a successful and universally appreciated product manager requires the right attitude and emotional intelligence at the right time.

If a person does not understand this, he will not be able to become a great product manager as he desires. Therefore, this book is dedicated to those who are aspiring to become a product manager who is a great company fit in all aspects. And for those who wants to become that perfect product manager in every way.

The book is about my own experience in taking on a product management role using my interpersonal and professional skills, and subsequently taking courses and certifications to improve my knowledge.

Writing a book is tougher than I thought and more gratifying than I could have ever imagined.

This book would not have been possible without the insights and mentoring of numerous people I have met along my professional journey. I have learned at least one thing from each of them, and therefore I am able to share so many of my learnings and knowledge through this book. I would like to extend my sincere thanks to all of them who allowed me to work with them and lead the emerging leaders.

WHY

An intriguing and common question, "WHY". However, when it comes to getting a sincere answer to anything, from your life to your office project, "why" is key.

Let's start with a question, why do you want to become a product manager or why did you choose product management as a career path?

Take your time to think, but the goal should be to have a clear and concise answer, not for me, of course, but for yourself.
Until you are satisfied with your answers, don't stop, keep asking why.
I got many answers for myself like, I wanted to get rid of core technical work, I didn't like coding, I wanted to manage people, I wanted more power to take any decision, etc.
But my why stopped when I realized I wanted to server customers more closely, understand their problems directly from them, and build solutions that target their real problems. Product management can give me that exposure and opportunity where I can connect with the company's customers to know their viewpoints. Hence, I wanted to become a product manager.

Be stubborn on vision but flexible on details". – Jeff Bezos.

My vision got clear, and I revisit this always and every day.

Therefore, I recommend, asking WHY to yourself before you get into this role or if you are already in it, to confirm your presence in this role. Ensure yourself what will you achieve getting into this, or did you achieve what you wanted from this role.

Let's talk now from the product manager's perspective. There is another very important decision that a product manager has to make.

WHY This Product?
Probably this question should echo in a product manager's mind throughout till his product is living. This question originates from the point when a product manager is at the very first stage of his journey.

That is, talking to his client or customers about their problems. This is where a product manager starts.
Before building any product, a product manager has to be sure of 2 things

- First, Why is he building this product - Building a product or enhancing a product to mimic competitors or because 'technology' is trending or any such weak foundation will lead him to crumble later on.

A product manager at this stage focuses on grasping and collecting as many problems as possible that his end users are suffering from. Collection of problems will not only help him understand his end users, but also get to know the customer's sentiments for his company, his product, and his services. The more he digs into the problems of the customer, the more it becomes easier to target that core problem which will solve other smaller issues along the way and lead to larger satisfaction.

A sensible understanding of the problem should be the outcome of this process, where the product manager is convinced enough to say, that "Yes, this is a genuine problem that needs a solution."

There is another perspective to this step, it also proves that there is no other better way to solve this problem than this product. A close look at how customers are dealing with these problems?, Is there any alternative that they can take? Is there any workaround? Or is it ok for them to live with this problem, as it is not that urgent? All these kinds of important research with the customer will help product managers to build a connection with their customers too.

- Second, for whom are we building this product –

Product managers are recommended to do user research to understand the target audience's mindsets, motivations, and behaviors. Figure out patterns in user research data that make it possible to categorize the users. Now, describe each persona in such a way that expresses enough understanding and empathy for that category. Finally, add life to the persona by relating it to a scenario or an imagined situation that describes how a persona would interact with a product in a particular context to achieve its end goal(s).

Until a product manager knows his customer or ends users, he will not be able to design his products as required. A lack of user knowledge will lead to building a product that is more relevant to the product manager's interest or developers' convenience.

Do you know other benefits of understanding your users?

Product managers usually work in multidisciplinary teams, where team members may have varying expertise, experience, and points of view. In such a scenario, creating a user persona or a character representing his customers will help everyone to relate with his customers. Hence, he has made it easy for everyone on his team to understand his customer and channel their thoughts and ideas toward his customers and not to their individual understanding.

A product manager's responsibility does not limit to only his customers, but also to other teams in his organization who are directly or indirectly related to his product. Understanding users or their problems alone will not help the product manager to achieve what he seeks. Onboarding his organization, developers, sponsors, leaders, marketers, etc to his idea is necessary to create a closed team who can relate themselves to the product manager's idea.

So, it is equally important to know for whom we are building the product along with understanding why we are building the product.

Any guesses which is the staple method of SaaS "product teams" for WHY analysis around the world?

This goes without saying, "The 5 Whys technique" You would be amazed to see how seamlessly you uncover the actual root cause of the issue.

You will end up nowhere but to solve root problems rather than symptoms. And unknowingly, you foster cross-functional collaboration, innovation and encourage a holistic approach to problem-solving techniques in your team.

Let's see how this mom discovered the reason why his son's lunch box wasn't finished.

> Mom's problem: Why you did not finish your lunch
> Son: I was not that hungry
>
> Mom: Why(1) were you not hungry
> Son: I had a burger on the way to school
>
> Mom: Why(2) did you have a burger on the way to school
> Son: I did not have breakfast in the morning
>
> Mom: Why(3) you did not have breakfast in the morning
> Son: I was getting late for school
>
> Mom: Why(4) were you getting late to school
> Son: I woke up late in the morning
>
> Mom: Why(5) you woke up late
> Son: Because I was playing PS3 late at night

There you are.

Lunch box back to home with food is rooted in PS3 late at night. This was a fun demonstration of 5whys' function. Trust me it is real fun wherever and anywhere you apply it.

It is very natural that while listening to your customers, you get bombarded with a list of problems. And believe me, this is a very good sign of a dependable and approachable product manager.

However, the product manager at this point needs to be intellectually disciplined to skillfully pick those problems which actually need to be solved for the success of his customer and organization.

There are many strategies/ways to identify problems a product manager want to solve.
He may consider a problem that impacts a majority of customers or a problem that is very urgent to solve and is badly impacting or a problem that can be solved with existing resources and align with our organization's goals etc.

Keeping aside all the tools and skills required to identify the problem, if we talk about the real agenda of the product manager, and what should be going on in his mind at this stage, it should be, to seek out that pain point which if solved leads to maximum satisfaction to customers. And, at the same time, it gives maximum success to his organization in terms of revenue, acclaim, competitive advantage, and brand building.

Since a Product manager belongs to both customer and the organization, this is the call he must make with an attitude to serve both parties emphatically.

Quoting Michael Porterer.
"The essence of strategy is choosing what not to do"

In conclusion, a Product manager works closely with the customers, sales, marketing, and engineering teams for various aspects. Hence the art, attitude, and sentiments of a product manager should be streamlined to better understand user problems and align the team with his ideas and the organization's goals.

2 IDEATION

Now that a product manager has understood the user problem and the root cause of it, he would want to rev up his idea generation engine and start thinking of ways the product team could address that need.

Recommended is to capture ideas on his own first before he enlists the help of his team. This helps him connect himself with the problem more.

It is a very interesting stage where the product manager can be himself and stimulate his "creativity glands" to bring out new and original ideas.

He knows his customers better, he knows the problems better, so it's time to exploit his apprehensions.

There can be many ways to challenge his knowledge and come up with new ideas by
- Talking to the sales team
- Reading the competitors' product reviews
- Conducting user surveys

- Reading what users say about the organization/product

And the, product manager can choose to do a group activity with his team, so everyone gets an opportunity to stretch themselves creatively and let their creative juices flow, hence, opening up the doors to true innovation.

This is also an opportunity for a product manager to create an environment in his team that allows them to venture beyond their individual areas of expertise. He can challenge the participants with multiple different scenarios to help them break free from the status quo, think out of the box and target the problem from new angles.

While choosing the participants, a product manager can let in a range of people from some old timers that know everything to some young blood to challenge assumptions and ask uncomfortable questions. However, the intention should be to keep the audience diverse, with representatives from each department or business function. It's also vital that everyone feels comfortable stepping outside their comfort zone and contributing ideas and that is why too many folks from any department are not suggested which may overshadow underrepresented cohorts.

Let's say a problem of the low number of downloads of a mobile app. In the ideation session, a product manager can get multiple viewpoints from multiple different perspectives. Like, a developer can suggest ways to make the app more user-friendly, a sales executive can suggest a better go-to-market strategy or a management leader can suggest better lucrative offers to accelerate the download rate.

Here, the product manager should accept the fact, that these ideas might by and large end up getting little-to-no consideration. Yet, during ideation, everything gets a square deal, and everyone has an opportunity to share their suggestions with the group. Inadvertently, the product manager establishes a platform from where he can reach to an unexpected conclusions and consensus.

A smart product manager should realize the hidden advantage of this process. It's a perfect way and ideal time to get the relevant stakeholders and management focused on this product. He can pull in a pool of stakeholders and participants to soak them in user research and feedback. This also helps everyone to be genuinely bought in for this product and not simply push their pet projects.

However, throughout this session, the product manager should ensure that his purpose to solve the problem is much clear to the ideation cohort so that it puts everyone in a mindset of trying to identify what would best fit. And then, the ideas that look promising after a few evaluations make their room into the idea backlog or directly to the product roadmap.

Hence an upbeat product manager should be sentimentally appreciative. He should assure that, participants in the ideation process should feel energized to see their ideas become part of the product strategy and path forward for the product and business.

3 STRATEGY

A Vision without a strategy remains an illusion – Lee Bolman
And a Product manager cannot believe in the illusion.

Most companies create a corporate vision, which is the highest-level view of what or where the company wants to be. Where vision could be more of an imaginary yet ambitious statement to inspire employees and customers, a strategy must be more calculated. For a product manager, this vision is his bull's eye. To get to that target, the product manager has to make a strategy.

As the name implies, strategy - this step is to carefully plan the actions to achieve a long-term or overall aim. Strategy is a high-level plan which documents real actions and represents accomplishable outcomes.

Strategizing a product is a very crucial part of the product manager's role. This piece of documentation is a way for a product manager to convey his product to all those who are directly or indirectly related to it.

A product manager with a solid goal and who is willing to experiment can create a well-defined strategy. A well defines strategy should be self-sufficient to speak about the product and how it will progress toward the organization goal.

Let's see what a well defines strategy consists of

Vision –
Vision is a heart of an organization to pump a purpose to everything else it does. A vision statement describes where an organization is going and what it will look like when it gets there. It communicates organization's value and commitment to achieving its goals.

Example: Ben & Jerry's: vision statement says: "Making the best ice cream in the nicest possible way."
This one-liner should be the goal of all the innovations that happen with ice creams at "Ben & Jerry".
Product managers rely on the organization's vision to make a product strategy.

Purpose –
This describes the problem. The problem that the customer is facing, and which has been

selected to pay attention to. The purpose drives the features of the product.

Hence all the stakeholders need to be aligned on the purpose of the product and be aware of it as development progresses to avoid any scope kill or scope creep.

Customers/Users –

The product strategy should clearly define, which user persona will be benefited from this product. To rephrase, these are the target audience, or customers of this product. The Product Manager would have already done this research while researching the problem (Refer to ch.1)

Specifying personas here will connect and act as a bridge between purpose and product.

Product –

This space is dedicated to describing the product. This is basically the output of the ideation process, refined to present in form of a product.

It should explain how this product fits into the larger ecosystem, determining where it adds value and where friction points remain.

What are the highlights of this product and how does it align with the goals and vision of the organization?

Product Vision –

This is a high-level long-term goal that the product is envisioned to achieve. The purpose of this section is to remind all stakeholders like the product team, development, executive staff, marketing, etc., about the common objective they're trying to achieve with this product.

Success Criteria –
This is the quantitative measurement of achievement. Product managers are required to call out different criteria which if achieved marks the success of the product. Example: SC#1: Feature 1 of product XYZ is completed within the given amount of budget of $1M. It is considered good for a product manager to keep metrics as closely aligned as possible to both customer success and business success.

Competitive edge/Alternative solution –
This critical section to assert what uniqueness the product manager wants to bring to this product or solution. Since it's a crowded market, products can more easily mimic each other in terms of their attributes and offered benefits. Product managers have to be creative enough to maintain a competitive edge. However, I would like to highlight what

is not considered to be a competitive edge. Product managers should keep in mind those areas, that does not set them apart from their competition. Ex: Quality of the product, Customer service, Price, or categories of product.

For a product manager, a product strategy document is a living document that grows as his product grows. It is a platform created by the product manager to get feedback and reiterate the document to mark what is working and what is not.

Product Manager must start every idea design project by defining the experience that he wants people to have with his product or service. Product strategy should be his primary tool to justify those user experience decisions. It will make him focus on achieving the ultimate goal, delivering the right features with the right user experience for the right people.

To conclude, setting a product strategy is not easy, and as I already mentioned, it is the most critical step in the product lifecycle.

The aim of a product manager is to make sure the product turns to be that what exactly product strategy is.

For a well-planned product manager, the school of thought should be to prepare a :
- Strategy on how the organization's business objectives connect with its product.
- Strategy to define product goals throughout its life cycle and how they will support the organization's goals.

4 ROADMAP

Where Strategy defines the direction the product manager will take to achieve his vision, roadmap captures activities the product manager will complete within a given time frame to reach the goal.

The purpose of strategy is to align the entire organization around what the product manager wants to accomplish and serves as a guide for how to turn the vision into reality. Roadmap can be used as a guide for prioritizing work, allocating resources, tracking dependencies, and communicating upcoming work in one view.

A library of roadmap templates are freely available to download and use, for almost all the categories, like marketing roadmap, DevOps roadmap, IT Architecture roadmap, etc.

However, a product manager should ensure the following common objectives are achieved through his roadmap across all domain

- It should clearly reflect how the strategy will be executed

- It should help to get all internal stakeholder alignment

- It should facilitate discussion of options and scenario planning

- It should ease communication with external stakeholders and customers

"You can't build a great building on a weak foundation" - Gordon B. Hinckley

If a product manager's vision and strategy have been articulated clearly, it becomes easier to create a roadmap that can secure executive buy-in effortlessly.

A product manager needs to have a clear understanding of why a roadmap is important for him. The very first point to keep in mind is product roadmaps are one of the few things almost everyone in the organization will be exposed to, such as sales pitches, marketing plans, and financials.

So, it should be created in a way that provides a shared, common understanding of the vision, goals, and objectives for everyone in the company.
Roadmap encapsulates many competing priorities to highlight what's most important against other shiny objects.

Hence, the intention behind creating a roadmap should be to create an intelligible order of work in the direction of the ultimate goal that product manager is trying to achieve and keep it clear of any undeserving inclusions.

Product roadmaps also help organizations avoid chaos among leaders to support their pet projects in between your implementation plan or utilizing resource efforts for something not important in your roadmap.

Therefore, a Product manager should be mindful while creating a roadmap to prepare in a way that becomes the radar, the focus, and the rule of thumb for everyone to bring the product to market.

Once the "Why" becomes clear, the "How" becomes easy. The backing contents for an out-and-out Product roadmap are
-	GOAL
-	FEATURES

- EPICS
- STORIES

To begin with, for creating a product roadmap, with a clear understanding of both the product's and the overall organization's strategic objectives, the product manager must outline the goals with timelines.
Goals are based on market problems you plan to solve. So, in simple words, put down which problems you will solve in what timeframe.

Now come features. First question that comes to mind, How do you prioritize features for the product roadmap?
There are myriads of frameworks to choose, from using OKRs to MoSCow, to the RICE Scoring Model. However, my aim isn't to teach the standard methods that are readily available everywhere to learn from.
Whichever tool we use, whatever method we follow,
our objective should be common.
Firstly, to figure out features that deserve a slot in the roadmap and keep riff-raff at bay. It's not a good idea to act on gut feelings or hunches at this stage. Well-documented facts and metrics should be available to support the shortlisted features and that they have value and best fit the final goal.

Secondly, features that have made the cut, in what order need to be executed with respect to time.

Look at your features through a more objective lens and cross-examine them through multiple views like:

- Viability - Talk to relevant executives and other product managers to understand how this feature works in a bigger ecosystem which consists of both your own strategies and goals and the industry as a whole, it's regulations, legal issues, and financials.

- Desirability – How much this feature is desired by your customers on a scale of 10. By talking to your researchers, and marketers, or performing any user tests might help in getting you the score.

- Feasibility – Talk to your technical team members like back-end engineers, UI designers, and front-end developers to understand how technically possible is the feature with given resources and technology. This will help to decontaminate what can be done from what's impossible or improbable.

Till here, the Roadmap is common for executives and Engineers. Based on the audience identified for your roadmap, you need to diverge your information from this point.

Roadmaps built for Executives must weigh on how your planned work will increase the value of the product and the company.

Do not lose sight of the fact that the executives product roadmap should exemplify how vital metrics that matter to the cohort are improved by these enhancements and developments.

Wherever applicable, try to keep the focus on strategic concepts such as driving growth, new market penetration, customer satisfaction, or market position.

A compassionate product manager should know that all the work individual contributors do often make sense within the context of the product roadmap only. Therefore, it is important for them to know the plan and what the organization hopes for. Therefore it will act as a source of inspiration, motivation, and shared ownership of the product and its successes. This will also drive to bring naysayers on board to product manager's objective.

5 PLANNING

As mentioned in the previous chapter, roadmaps built are different for a different audiences.
When the audience is the engineering team, it calls for a rigorous planning and detailing.
This can be achieved by creating a bridge between the high-level strategic goals and the actionable development tasks.

This bridge is called Epics.

An epic is an oeuvre that a product team creates as they break down a strategic goal into smaller initiatives. As an example, let's look at
GOAL: Increase the number of mobile app downloads
Epic 1: Simplify the download process
Epic 2: Send push notifications to potential target customers

As a product manager, it's your responsibility to write the epic and maintain its specs.
However, it's equally important to collaborate with the whole team. Engaging the engineering and

designing teams while formulating the epic will ensure that everyone involved understands the goal of the epic.

This is where intensive planning and discussion are required between the product team and development team to come to a common consensus of what, how, and when.

This is the stage where the first-time developers and product managers work so closely together to push out darn good products.

Hence, a product manager along with focusing on his own product knowledge and functional skills should also be attentive to communicating and collaborating with developers that'll make his relationship with them more productive and harmonious.

Planning and creating epics together can be considered one of the many ways to build a positive relationship and establish a common ground of understanding between both parties. The other approach to looking at epics is, as it is a group of organized tasks and a hierarchy in the development process, connected to the larger goal.

Epics break down development work into shippable components while keeping the daily tasks connected to the larger goal.

Let's recall previous example and talk about Epic 1
GOAL: Increase the number of mobile app downloads
Epic 1: Simplify the download process

Tasks to simplify the download process
1. Reduce app size
2. Easy sign-up synced with Google credentials

Any guesses what these tasks 1 & 2 are called? Did I hear, User Stories? Yes, you are right.

User stories are the smallest piece of tasks in the agile framework. These are the actionable items that consequently and collectively lead us to our strategic goal.

For a product manager, the agenda of the planning phase should be to avoid conflicts and misunderstandings in the development process. And that is why it is important to abide by a common format or structure while documenting an Epic or User Story.

Epic –
Epic always has a name. A clear, concise title reduces confusion and miscommunication among the team.
Followed by a narrative of the epic. A narrative

can be a long write-up or a short script but should have the following details to make it useful

1. Who: Mention the persona who has requested the objective.
2. What: The objective to be achieved in this Epic
3. Why: the value behind the objective, or the Goal

As the product manager [Who], I want to simplify the download process of the app [What] so that we increase the number of app downloads [Why].

This completes your Epic, however, additional information in the epic is not a sin. You can add some more information that strongly justifies this epic like your research or feedback from customers justifying download process concerns.

The epic writing phase is concluded. You are now ready for the next stage: User stories.
It's tempting to think that user stories are, simply put, software system requirements. But they're not.

User stories descend from Epic and that is why it contains the flavor of Epic. User story puts end users at the center of the conversation. And that is why the template goes like

1. Who - Who are we building this for?

2. Wants to - Describing their intent and what is it they're actually looking for.
3. So that – clarifies what's the overall benefit they're trying to achieve

Let's recall the above example
Epic 1: Simplify the download process
Task1: Reduce the mobile app size
As a interested app user, I want to see a smaller size app, so that it can be downloaded quickly consuming fewer network data.

This kind of user story structure defines done. When that persona can capture their desired value, the story can be marked as done or complete.

However, even after this, an unexpected result at the end of a development stage is inevitable.
To avoid it, acceptance criteria can be added to the user story to ensure that all stakeholders and users are satisfied with what they get.
The most commonly used scenario-based acceptance criteria acts as a clear indicator for developers while testing, when to begin and when to end the testing of a particular feature.

The template of an acceptance criteria follows

Given/When/Then sequence as
- Given a customer wants to download the app, when he searches for the app in the play store, then he should be able to see the app along with the app size within 50MB
- Given customer decided to download the app, when he clicks on the download button, then the app should not take more than 10 seconds to download.

This example of acceptance criteria is making the feature scope more detailed, setting a synchronous communication between the client and development team, and also helping in feature evaluation.

I conclude this chapter with a few important tips to help mobile product manager set up a productive relationship with the development team.
- Coffee breaks together – Get to know each other, and share what's cooking in the product kitchen.
- Know work specifications – Save each other's time and annoyance by knowing about each other professionally and personally to extend possible.
- Lose expectation of 100% - Product managers being obsessed about having it all at the same time will restrict dev creativity to find alternatives. Expectations should be given some

time.

- Two-way street communication – Dictating requirements on dev will never work out. A virtuous relationship demands listening to feedback, answering questions, and compromising that works for both parties

- Make them believe in you – The product manager can try to match his questions with their expertise and try to get to the stage where they can share their ideas freely.

Therefore, A harmonious and supportive relationship between the product and development team is the driving factor of the planning process and a propitious outcome too.

6 DESIGN & DEVELOPMENT

While the product manager is not developing the product directly, it would not be wrong to say, that product managers must be more heedful and involved in this phase.

A designer designs all the flows of your product. From happy flows to errors and edge cases. They ensure that the interaction design is correct and that the interface appears clear and intuitive. In addition, they need to write the text and select the right words for the interface. Their goal is to translate the solution to a real screen that gives the user an excellent experience.

For a product manager, the trick to getting the winning design out from designers is by communicating clearly and transparently.

The product manager's responsibility at this stage is to make sure product designers are well aware of the following
- Metrics to measure success: Explain how to know the product is successful. What are the numbers the company hopes to achieve?

- Product goal and product vision: What the product intends to solve, and "why are we doing this?" are questions that he must explain to designers so they can understand the "WHY" behind the work.

- Product roadmap and product strategy: They need to know where they are going and what problems they will address in the future. If not explained clearly, they may get surprises in each sprint regarding what they need to consider.

- Conversations in data and "Why": Let us understand this with an example. If the product manager has to communicate a scenario where redesigning is required, there could be 2 ways

1. We need to redesign the mobile app download process next week.

OR

2. Next week we need to work on a new mobile app download process because the number of users that uninstalled the app increased by 40% in the last 3 months.

Which one seems more effective?

The second way is the correct way and is expected from a product manager. This let the designer add relevant value and ideas.

Constant collaboration with designers will add efficiency during the designing phase. In the event when you notice that things are not working well and that the responsibilities are unclear, setting up a meeting and talking directly make things better.

A frequent feedback loop is the best way to keep teams aligned with the requirements. Giving good or bad feedback to designers will make them think of things they didn't previously consider to improve the solution.

As much as a product manager is confident in his functional knowledge of the product, with the same intensity, he must be empathetic to his designers. The conflict situation arises when the product manager tends to decide without considering the designer's say.

An overachiever product manager invites designers as early stage as possible. Similarly, notify the designers as quickly as possible if he finds that things are not clearly understood by the other side.

Similarly, for a product manager to work with developers, it requires him to be available and approachable whenever required.
While the planning stage has already set the rhythm, now during the development phase, the product manager has to keep himself ready for the releases and feedback sessions.

With the industry moving towards agile

methodology, the release cycle has been reduced to a much shorter duration. This keeps the product manager as well as the development team quite active and iterative in the process.

Once the Product manager defines the minimum viable product (MVP), and the MVP is released, a product manager sets up a feedback collection process. Based on the gathered feedback, product requirements are altered corresponding to user input.

The feeling of a student getting exam results is the same as a developer getting customer feedback on the piece of development he has worked on in a release. The product manager facilitates the tests, where user gets the access to run the product and test the application through multiple scenarios.

A product manager has to coordinate with potential customers making sure that they will be honest about the usability of a product. While testing, the product manager analyses the user reaction and the customers' feedback. With all the analysis reports, the product manager, goes back to the eagerly waiting developers for the results. Consequently, developers can prepare the software for launch or introduce changes to the existing product. Result be anything, the product manager should make sure the team spirits do not go down and they are appreciated for their efforts. With tight deadlines and the creativity for solving problems, it isn't always free-flowing. However, when developers are motivated, they can manage all of that much more smoothly.

An inspiring product manager makes sure the development team is motivated and rewarded. Give them the freedom to do what they do best and trust them. Developers value their skills, and it's important and inspiring if the product manager also values them. Drive the developers towards the latest technology, preventing their skills from becoming obsolete. Challenge them with new and complex ideas to motivate them to do their job to the best of their abilities, thus increasing their engagement and paving the path to mastery.

7 LAUNCH

A product launch is a process to bring a new or updated product to market.

Here is the final stage to announce a new or improved product to the world and to your potential customers.

It would not be wrong to say that a product manager's first product launch is often his most difficult. That is because product launch is not an individual process, it requires the alignment of members of a product team with other departments to ensure the entire business is unified in its approach to support the new product.

Ideally, planning for a product launch begins while the product itself is still in development. The features planned to include in a launch version of the product may fundamentally change or disappear in the development phase. Similarly, any hitch while development may affect the launch date and schedule. So, the planning of the launch is one important area the product manager should focus along with keeping the development team updated in the development phase.

According to the Businesswire report released on September 09, 2019, 12:02 PM Eastern Daylight Time –
"Gartner Survey Finds That 45% of Product Launches Are Delayed by at Least One Month"

Iterative development, collaboration, testing, and sudden change to the approach in marketing midway are a few of the reasons that might derail launch plans.

For a product manager to build a successful launch strategy, can follow some of the tips.
- Revolve around the customer:
The product manager should make sure that before planning a launch, the following questions have clear answers laid down.
1) Why customers will use the product
2) What problem this product is solving
3) How is the product different from existing competitions
- Use the testing results to prepare the launch strategy:
This involves analytics on observations collected by product managers while the customer was testing the product. Let's understand it with an example-
While Beta testing, you observed customers

were mostly using the camera feature of your app. Then what, it would make sense for your marketing communication to emphasize the camera feature to attract customers with a higher likelihood for engagement from the get-go. And you just realized, you killed two birds with one stone.

- Product launch checklist:

It's easy for even the most organized person to lose track of what needs to get done while handling an ever-changing list of tasks. Hence, keeping a running list of all essential tasks ensures that nothing falls between the cracks as the launch day nears. Therefore, a running checklist is an essential component of a product launch. Items should be checked off as they're done or appended as new ideas or complications arise.

The common yet most crucial items to be checked before product launch are:

- ☑ Create a product launch schedule
- ☑ Identify relevant KPIs to measure the success
- ☑ Define target audience
- ☑ Choose distribution channels
- ☑ Craft the right marketing message

Normally, the launch process takes several months, and even the formal release of your new product to the public spans longer than a single day.

As already mentioned, it's not a single person's

responsibility. Marketing efforts like social media posts and email campaigns should be focused enough days before the product is released, as information often takes time to spread.
correspondingly, the agenda of launch teams should be to focus on building buzz ahead of the launch and maintaining momentum in the days and weeks following an official launch day.

Again, waiting for exam results is the only feeling which cannot be expressed in words. The product manager is in the same situation during the launch.

But I recommend, the best way to live with this situation is to prepare for good or bad.
Since these exam results do not have grades, why not create own scale to measure success and failure? This not only helps him to prepare for ongoing launches but also for future launches so, they can be optimized for success.
Some of the scales of success measurement are:
- Change in web traffic after product launch
- Raise in revenue amount after the launch
- Leads generated, customer usage and retention, and how many trial user signed it.
As the above focus on a quantitative measure of product success, it is equally important, to know how well the product and messaging were received by the customers. Simple ways to do it are by

- Customers interview to know their reaction to the product
- Focus group to see to what extent the product was able to solve the problem we intended to.
- Surveys to understand the market reaction as a group on the new product.

While everyone's focus during a product launch is on customers and end users, a product manager should equally focus on how well the product launch went within his company.

There could be so many points of friction arising for various reasons before and after launch.

Let's say, the customer service team interacts with customers during the launch. They may have unique insights into issues or concerns that arose through customer requests. Also, other teams may have figured out issues in the internal process that your team is not aware of. A number of similar scenarios arising in the organization after launch also contribute to the score of launch success.

In the end, a prudent product manager with his launch team should work with an attitude to create coordination of all the involved teams—product management, sales, marketing, development, customer success, etc. So that, all the team feels they are aligned to a common goal and working toward agreed-upon milestones.

Reiterating, a product launch is not a single-person job, product manager should majorly focus on ensuring the product launch is smooth and creating the maximum positive impact in the market.

8 EPILOGUE

I started this book with a basic question: "Why". After reading this, I hope you would have understood the importance of this word.
It's not just a word, but a curiosity to know the problem, to understand the problem in a better way as possible. This is the foundation of whatever you plan to do next.

Having set the foundation, the next chapter talks about how you convert that problem into a creative solution for your customers.
Your zeal to solve user problems and serve your organization comes out in form of various ideas. These ideas are small packets of innovations that go through multiple filters and come out refined which are the castings for the further steps

In the third chapter, these castings are then used to lay down a plan of action. Your art of planning and directing reaches its peak and a well-defined strategy is created to align these ideas with the overall organization's goals.

With an approved strategy, you move ahead to the fourth chapter to create a roadmap for your product. Executive's assent, development & technical team buy-in, and other stakeholders' attention on your product become the supporting factor of your roadmap.

Further ahead from the roadmap takes you to a phase of collaboration with the development team. In the fifth chapter, we talked about planning where you work with the development team to create technical documents and align the technical team to your strategic goal and purpose.

Then starts the designing and development process in the sixth chapter. Your role to keep the team aligned with your goals is one of the many responsibilities you need to play. Your duty to keep the team motivated and supportive to let creativity slip in while creating solutions for your product becomes a crucial part of your role.

Finally, when the product is ready to launch, in the seventh chapter, we saw how the product manager can handle efficiently, the most dynamic and iffy phase, which is the product launch phase.

And at the same time, evaluates the success of the launch both externally and internally.

Every chapter ends with a note that depicts what should be the sentiments and attitude of a product manager in each stage of the product lifecycle.

Please note, the role of product management spans many activities from strategic to tactical, some very technical, others less so. It differs from organization to organization and from product to product. All the seven stages mentioned above may not be performed by a single product manager or may have a dedicated team to perform.

This book is not to teach the standard process and methodologies of product management, which are easily available for everyone to learn. The motive of this book is to share the personal experience of being a product manager. What, a product manager deals with psychologically and how his attitude needs to be blended with the flavors of each different stage.

ABOUT THE AUTHOR

This is my first book based on Product Management. I am married to my childhood friend and am a mother of a little bud. I have been a software engineer, a product manager, and an occasional social media user.

I graduated as an engineer and have been working in the IT industry for the past 11 years. I am a self-motivated learner who loves to empower others with my knowledge and expertise.

www.ingramcontent.com/pod-product-compliance
Lightning Source LLC
Chambersburg PA
CBHW071122240526
45465CB00022B/781